IMAGES OF ENGLAND

SUTTON PARK

IMAGES OF ENGLAND

SUTTON PARK

MARIAN BAXTER

TEMPUS

First published 2006

Tempus Publishing Limited
The Mill, Brimscombe Port,
Stroud, Gloucestershire, GL5 2QG
www.tempus-publishing.com

© Marian Baxter 2006

The right of Marian Baxter to be identified as the Author
of this work has been asserted in accordance with the
Copyrights, Designs and Patents Act 1988.

All rights reserved. No part of this book may be reprinted
or reproduced or utilised in any form or by any electronic,
mechanical or other means, now known or hereafter invented,
including photocopying and recording, or in any information
storage or retrieval system, without the permission in writing
from the Publishers.

British Library Cataloguing in Publication Data.
A catalogue record for this book is available from the British Library.

ISBN 0 7524 4069 1
Typesetting and origination by Tempus Publishing Limited.
Printed in Great Britain.

Contents

Acknowledgements

My thanks go to the following people: Dr M.A. Hodder; R. Lea, Bernard R. Haynes and Dr John Raines who lent photographs included in this publication – Dr Raines also allowed me to use the programme for the Bertram Mills Circus; Robert Pritchard, who allowed me to use the N.G. Evans Collection and photograph; Maureen Williams, who allowed me to use her late husband K.J. Williams' collection and photographs on the mills of Sutton Coldfield; John C.W. Field, who not only entrusted me with his vast collection of Sutton Park postcards but also helped put together the chapter on military use of Sutton Park. Finally, my thanks go to Brian M. Hall MLS MCLIP for proofreading the text.

Longmoor Pool, *c*. 1950.

Introduction

Sutton Park National Nature Reserve lies to the west of Sutton Coldfield and approximately seven miles from Birmingham. It has been described as 'a jewel in the crown' and 'a Park for all People'. It is both of these and much more.

Apart from the *Sutton Park Guide,* which was rewritten in 2001, there has not been a book published about the Park since 1982, nor has a photographic book ever been produced. The problem with putting this book together is not what could be put in, but what would have to be left out. Sutton Park is a unique and special place which should be shared, and I apologise for the areas not covered in this volume.

Sutton Park is the largest local authority park of its type in this country. Covering some 2,400 acres, it has a seven-mile perimeter within which landscape features include woodlands, heathland, wetlands and marshes and seven pools, all with their own histories and varieties of wildlife and plants.

The Park is a remnant of an extensive forest that used to cover much of the Midlands. It has retained many ancient features, including prehistoric mounds and a barrow as well as a Roman road and other archaeological remains, giving it a fascinating history.

The variety of plant life in the Park supports a vast number of common and rare insects and invertebrates, and the make-up of the Park attracts many species of birds which travel great distances to and from the site. The seven pools cover about seventy acres and the marshes 300 acres. The pools support an array of algae, water plants, bog plants and submerged water vegetation which provide a prolific source of food for the fish. The woodlands, which cover about 550 acres, are semi-natural; many of them have had new species introduced over the years. Their shape and size is a result of being fenced, coppiced and grazed. The dry heathland represents one of the largest areas of heathland in the Midlands. Today it is a result of low-key grazing since the twelfth-century and many of the rodents and mammals are totally dependent upon the vegetation of these areas.

It is hard to imagine today that in its early history Sutton Park was a place which was exploited by man. It was a place where cattle were brought in, a place where people would come and collect firewood, harvest the heather and the gorse, and harvest berries for food. It was not a place where people would go walking, cycling, horse riding, fishing for pleasure, sailing, jogging or kite flying. The recreational use of Sutton Park only came about in Victorian times.

The survival of the Park is even more remarkable in that today it is on the edge of a large urban conurbation, and completely encircled by development. It should be remembered that the Park is essentially man-made and is not the wholly natural feature which it is often assumed to be.

Sutton Park has an estimated 2.5 million visitors a year, which does put pressure on its environment. Yet despite the problems associated with urban fringe and antisocial behavior, there is still the superb and spectacular diversity of its natural and colourful history which combine to make it a site of national importance. It was designated as a Site of Special Scientific Interest under the National Parks and Access to the Country Act (1949) in 1954 and was renotified in 1987 under the Wildlife and Countryside Act (1981). In April 1997 the Park received its new status when English Nature, the agency responsible for the wildlife and nature conservation in England, awarded it the status of a National Nature Reserve. In addition, it is included on English Heritage's list of historic parks and gardens in recognition of its historic and landscape features. This is why Sutton Park is a park for all people and a jewel in the crown.

one

Archaeology

Aerial view of Sutton Park, showing the Roman Road. It is hard to imagine that thousands of years ago people were hunting wild animals, living off the plants and fishing in what is now Sutton Park. They would have been nomadic herdsmen who may well have congregated and socialised in the Park.

The Roman Road, Sutton Park. Known as the Ryknield or Icknield Street, this road is one-and-a-half miles in length and was built as part of the Roman conquest of the West Midlands, just a few years after the Roman army landed in Kent in AD 43. The 112-mile-long road comes through Birmingham by way of Handsworth, Perry Barr and Kingstanding, and enters the Park near to the Banners Gate entrance. It crosses the bogs and heathland in Longmoor Valley and the golf course on the western side. It leaves on the Streetly side to run alongside the Roman Road on the Little Aston Park Estate, and then heads to Shenstone to join Watling Road, which is partly followed by the modern A5.

This military road joined the forts at Metchley (by the University of Birmingham), on Vincent Drive and the fort at Wall, near Lichfield. The Roman Road would not have had a paved surface. Excavations have shown that it consists of compacted gravel. The bank or agger would have been about eight metres wide, and alongside of the agger there is an intermittent ditch, which was a laying-out line dug by the Roman surveyors to mark where vegetation would have to be cleared to construct the road. It was not a drainage ditch, nor was it groove lines made from the passing of many cartwheels. Beyond the side ditches there are pits and hollows which show where the gravel was dug out some 2,000 years ago to make the road.

The Ancient Encampment is on a hill between Bracebridge and Blackroot Pools. It consists of earthworks (mounds and hollows). The date and purpose of the site are uncertain but the purpose of the site has been debated since the nineteenth century when, in 1880, Ebenzer Edwards provided the first reference to the earthworks. He described the site thus: 'the surface is entirely composed of ridges and depressions, arranged upon a systemic plan. This is a time-worn military encampment'. Midgley, writing in 1904, thought it had been scooped out by Celtic tribes. In 1906 Benton recorded masonry being unearthed in the bottom of a ditch during the construction of the railway in 1875. All of the maps after 1880 describe the site as the Ancient Encampment.

In 1999 Birmingham University Field Archaeological Unit carried out a dig and the survey was to cast doubt on the site being an Ancient Encampment. The group thought that the ditch may have been an old contour path, and the rest may well be linked to quarrying for sand. The sand may well have been used for either part of the railway construction or for the building of the nearby Four Oaks Park Estate.

The barrow is to be found within a small plantation known as Queens Coppice. Excavations in 1859 on the tumulus revealed very little except that the mound was artificial. Another survey in 1999 concluded that a 'contour survey has highlighted an interesting anomaly possibly encircling the site'. The conclusion was that 'although visually the site is difficult to interpret as a man-made mound, it does occupy an elevated position in relation to the surrounding topography, a practice typical of barrow builders'.

Quarry for a dam at Longmoor Pool, constructed in the eighteenth-century to drive a corn mill. Earth was dug from this pit to construct a dam across a small stream.

The remains of a laid hawthorn hedge on a bank with a ditch, forming the boundary of a field created near Longmoor Pool in the eighteenth century.

Lower Nut Hurst, Bishop Vesey Boundary. The present boundaries of Sutton Park correspond almost exactly to those of the twelfth-century deer park. In order to keep deer within reasonable bounds, deer parks were established within an area of about one square kilometer, and as the exclusive rules about who could hunt deer were relaxed, so every minor Baron wanted his own deer park. Deer parks were a status symbol and hunting was a favourite recreation. Also, the creation of a deer park made good economic use of poor agricultural land.

SUTTON PARK: Earthwork Enclosures

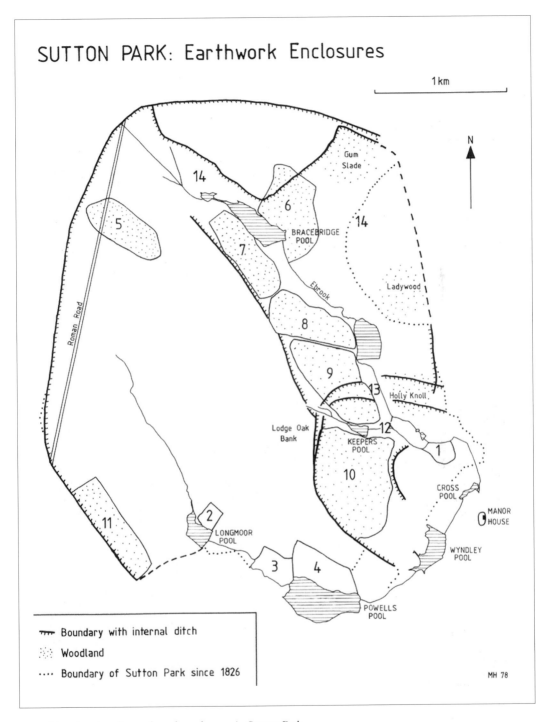

Map showing the earthwork enclosures in Sutton Park.

Alongside Streetly Lane, Thornhill Road and Chester Road there is a ditch inside the boundary, and the modern-day fence runs along a bank. The bank, ditch and a paling fence on the bank would have created a barrier that was too high and too wide for deer to jump over. Other banks and ditches subdivided the Park, such as those near to Keeper's Pool, which may have created smaller enclosures into which deer were led to make hunting easier.

Six mounds were exposed by fire on the Streetly Lane side of the Park in 1926. Excavation showed that each was composed of stones shattered by heating, and two of the mounds had pits under them. The mounds are similar to the burnt mounds found in other parts of Birmingham, which have been dated by the radiocarbon method to between 1500–100 BC. These sites were once thought to be the result of cooking using hot stones, but alternatively they could be the debris from sauna bathing using hot stones to produce steam.

two

Encroachments

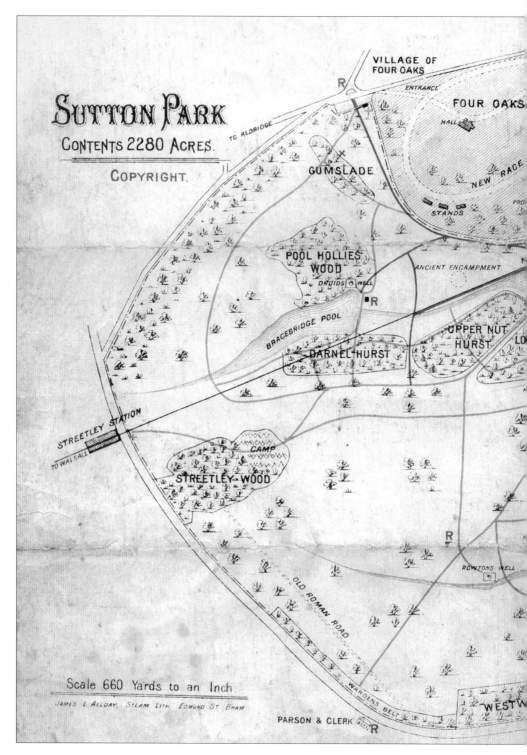

Map of Sutton Park 1894. It is not possible to define the original boundaries of Sutton Park at the time of the 1528 Charter. Maps were rare and it is likely that the boundaries were fixed more by

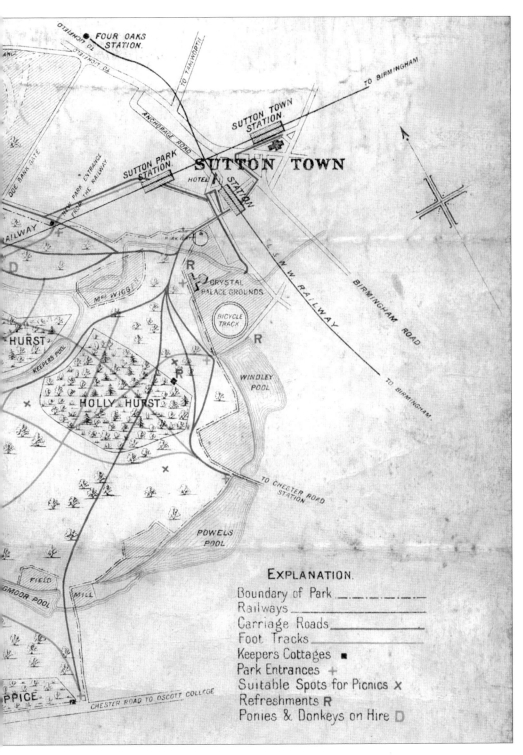

FOUR OAKS STATION.

TO LICHFIELD

TO TAMWORTH

TO BIRMINGHAM

ANCHORAGE ROAD

SUTTON TOWN STATION.

SUTTON PARK STATION.

PARK ENTRANCE FROM THE RAILWAY

SUTTON TOWN

HOTEL

STATION

DOE BANK GATE

RAILWAY

PARK GATE

D

R

CRYSTAL PALACE GROUNDS

Mrs WIGGS

BICYCLE TRACK

L N W RAILWAY

BIRMINGHAM ROAD

TO BIRMINGHAM.

HURST

KEEPERS POOL

R

R

WINDLEY POOL

HOLLY HURST

TO CHESTER ROAD STATION

POWELS POOL

FIELD

MILL

GMOOR POOL

PPICE

CHESTER ROAD TO OSCOTT COLLEGE

EXPLANATION.

Boundary of Park ___._.___._.___
Railways _____
Carriage Roads _____
Foot Tracks _____
Keepers Cottages ▪
Park Entrances +
Suitable Spots for Picnics x
Refreshments R
Ponies & Donkeys on Hire D

custom and by local memory than by written and drawn description. It is known that the Park has changed its shape over the years by adding and exchanging land.

Above: Four Oaks Hall, 1879. In 1827 Sir Edmund Hartopp, who then owned Four Oaks Hall, wished to enlarge the 1756 encroachment by taking another sixty-three adjoining acres. He exchanged land with the Warden and Society, receiving fifty-seven acres out of the Park. However, he gave up just over ninety-three acres, with fifty-one-and-a-half acres being added to the Park; thirty-six-and-a-half acres near Powell's Pool and fifteen acres on what is now known as Meadow Platt. The remaining forty-two acres on Tudor Hill were to provide an income for the Sutton Coldfield Muncipal Charities.

Opposite above: One of the pools in the ground behind Park House. The threat of encroachments is nothing new for Sutton Park. Not long after the death of Bishop Vesey, some of the inhabitants of Sutton Coldfield were allowed to carve out farms for themselves, one of the most obvious being Park House grounds, which was there in 1597, and in 1581 and 1617 Suttonians had to take to task their own Warden and Society for misappropriating land when some cottages within the Park had to be pulled down and the site returned to the wild.

Opposite below: In 1778 Sir Gilbert Scott of Great Barr set up a scheme to share all the 'waste', including Sutton Park, among the principal landowners. The townspeople successfully opposed that plan. When permission for enclosures was granted in 1825 the Park was left untouched. In 1756, Simon Luttrell, owner of Four Oaks Hall, evaded the purport of the Charter and obtained an Act of Parliament enabling him to extend his estate by taking forty-eight acres of Sutton Park, which adjoined his land, thus changing the shape of the Park forever.

Above: Driver under instruction – train passing Blackroot Pool, March 1961. In July 1866 the Corporation sold land to the Midland Railway Company, which was to become the site of the Sutton Park Station. In 1871, against much opposition, a new railway line was built through the Park. The passenger line from Water Orton to Walsall was closed in 1962 and is now used as a goods line only. This photograph was taken looking towards Streetly. Diesels of this type (Peaks) were soon to be used on NE/ SW trains passing through Birmingham. This locomotive (D21) was allocated to Saltley shed so that local drivers could gain experience in operating them. (Dr John Raines)

Opposite above: The main advantage to the inhabitants of Sutton Coldfield was that Sir Edmund Hartopp agreed to construct Park Road and a new main entrance to the Park (Town Gate) giving easier accessibility for horse-drawn vehicles who were finding the old entrance down the narrow steep Wyndley Lane more and more difficult.

Opposite below: This exchange was to have long-lasting effects on the Park. Before the Hartopp exchange the Park had been used for its timber, as a pasture for the local inhabitants' cattle and for hunting. The new easy access via Park Road soon brought horse-drawn carriages full of pleasure-seeking people from further afield. It was the beginning of Sutton Park being used for leisure and sporting activities.

Park Protection

Association

The burgesses of Sutton Coldfield are invited to air their views on the formation of the above Association in St. Peters Hall, Maney, on Friday 8th December, 1950 at 7-30 p.m.

If you do not wish the Park to be destroyed, you must attend this meeting and give your support to this proposal to ensure the future of your heritage.

Do not leave it to someone else.

You ARE someone else !

Chairman :   Mr. Kenneth C. Blacklock.

Randall Bros. (Printers) Ltd., Aston Cross, Birmingham, 6

Above: Some time around 1907 H.E.B. wrote *Hands off the Park.* Here are a few lines from that poem:

> In days gone by,
> There's been many a try.
> To steal our ancient right.
> But it always fails,
> And the Council quails,
> When the people start to fight!
> By ways that are dark,
> They would grab our Park,
> And make it a Penny Fair;
> With some roundabouts,
> And the booth-man's shouts,
> To pollute God's lovely air!
> 'Midst woodland scenes,
> They would put canteens,
> To attract the City crowds;
> And a cheap hotel,
> Might be built as well,
> If the Council were allowed!

Left: Poster advertising the setting up of the Park Protection Society.

HISTORY AND GUIDE

TO

SUTTON PARK,

BY

ABSALOM PEERS.

RULES & REGULATIONS.

CHARGES FOR ADMISSION.

On Mondays, Tuesdays, Wednesdays, Thursdays, and Saturdays, ... 1d.

On Fridays and Sundays,... ... ... 2d.

Children under seven, and Charity Schools, half-price.

For every Conveyance with one Horse ... 6d.

For every other Conveyance, per horse ... 6d.

For each Person on Horseback, ... 6d.

All strange Dogs found in the Park will be destroyed.

The sale of all articles in the Park is strictly prohibited.

No Fire to be lighted or Tents erected without special permission

Tickets of Admission to be produced to the Park Keepers on application, or the parties be re-charged.

All Persons committing any injury in the Park will be apprehended and prosecuted.

Bathing after nine in the morning is prohibited.

An Inspector and Body of Police will be employed to enforce the above Regulations.

PRICE ONE PENNY.

Rules and regulations from *History and Guide to Sutton Park* by A. Peers, 1869. In 1920 the Council withdrew a proposal to 'enable the Corporation to improve the Park and its lakes, roads and footpaths, to erect maintain and let pavilions, concert halls, reading and refreshments room, and charge admission thereto, to set apart portions of the park for golf, cricket, football and other games …' In 1923 people power again won the day when the Council of Public Health Amendment Act Part IV was not adopted. This would have meant various powers being granted to 'enclose during the time of frost any part or ground for the purpose of protecting ice for skating and charge admission … to enclose any part of the park or ground not exceeding one acre, for the convenience of persons listening to any band of music and charge admission … to place any persons to place chairs or tables and charge for the use of them … to set apart any such part of the park for the purposes of cricket, football, or any other game or recreation and to exclude the public from the part set aside while it is in actual use for that purpose' etc.

Powell's Pool. Another exchange was made in 1937 when the trustees of the Somerville Estates conveyed land to the Corporation enabling them to construct Monmouth Drive and brought Powell's Pool and Wyndley Pool into the Park.

Wyndley Pool.

three

The Woods of Sutton Park

Aerial view of Sutton Park. The woods of Sutton Park cover approximately 650 acres, one quarter of the total area. Much of the woodland is located in the northern part of the Park. The predominant trees are oak, birch, holly, beech, sweet chestnut, rowan, larch, and Scots pine. Today one sees the effects of deliberate planting in many of the woods.

Opposite below: Sixteenth-century boundary at Streetly Wood. Most of the woods are in the form of fenced and ditched enclosures, and many of the ditches are thought to be original boundary ditches made in the sixteenth century.

Westwood Coppice Boundary. When the Park became common grazing land as a result of the Royal Charter of 1528, its woodlands, the Seven Hayes, were protected from grazing animals with a bank and a ditch, a fence or a hedge on the bank. The bank and ditch can still be seen around Streetly Wood, Darnel Hurst, Pool Hollies, Upper and Lower Nut Hursts, and Holly Hurst. Most of Lady Wood is now outside the Park.

Sutton Park is often described as a 'natural' park but it is the result of thousands of years of human management. Most of the ancient parks were created for the conservation and the hunting of deer. Sutton Park is a remnant of the Forest of Kank (Cannock). There are few signs to indicate what trees originally grew there, and many of the woods we see today are the result of deliberate planting over the years.

Above: The wood would have been used for building and fuel, and pollarding and coppicing would have been carried out. The felling of trees is not new. Between 1726 and 1792, 15,382 oak trees were sold; in 1737, 3,700 trees from Holly Hurst; in 1759, 1,050 from the whole of the Park; in 1766, 1,635 from Nut Hurst; in 1770, 1,270 from Nut Hurst; in 1786, 120 from Darnel Hurst, 420 from Nut Hurst, 360 from Holly Hurst, and 120 from Pool Hollies. In 1789, 220 were sold from the Park and in 1792, 60 were sold from Streetly Wood.

Right: The names of some of the woods are descriptive, Holly Hurst and Pool Hollies reflecting the holly trees.

E Brook (Plants Brook) between Blackroot and Bracebridge Pools.

Left: Woods in Sutton Park.

Opposite above: Holly Hurst. The name of this wood indicates the most dominant tree, holly. Holly has been growing in the Park for many years and was distributed in bundles to the residents of Sutton Coldfield. However, the demand became so great that it had to be abandoned as being impractical in 1965.

Opposite below: Between 1902 and 1912 it was suggested that parts of Holly Hurst be replanted with Weymouth and Corsican pines. This was never carried out.

1895. SUTTON PARK. HOLLY HURST.

— In Sutton Coldfield Park —

"BABES IN THE WOOD"　　　SUTTON PARK

Looking from Holly Hurst to Keeper's Pool. The path above the pool and centre leads through Lower Nut Hurst.

Opposite above: According to *A Guide and History of Sutton Park*, written in 1965, the north-eastern half of Holly Hurst was known as Brown's Wood.

Opposite below: Upper and Lower Nut Hurst. It is possible that the name of the wood came about after the planting of the sweet chestnut. The area above Keeper's Pool was replanted in the 1930s with a mixture of larch, Scots pine, spruce, chestnut and oak, and a plantation in the centre of Nut Hurst was planted in the 1920s.

Woodland scene looking towards Blackroot Pool from Nut Hurst, 1887.

Nut Hurst, Sutton Coldfield.

Above: Nut Hurst.

Right: Wyndley Glade in winter, *c.* 1900.

Railway bridge in Darnel Hurst. 1887. Darnel Hurst as a name is more obscure, although darnal is a species of wild grass. The woods here are made up of thirty-three acres of varying woodland which Stony Glade separates from Upper Hut Hurst.

Bracebridge Woods – Pool Hollies. This wood is to be found on the north-eastern side of Bracebridge Pool, and like Holly Hurst, is noted for its holly.

In the woods. It looks like an interesting conversation.

Above: Pool Hollies. Path leading to Bracebridge Pool.

Right: Looking along the edge of Pool Hollies.

It is not clear where this lovers' walk is situated in Sutton Park.

People often count these bridges in Pool Hollies, but never get the same number twice.

GUM SLADE, SUTTON, COLDFIELD

The Gum Slade, 1887.

Opposite above: The Gum Slade. Some of the oldest trees in the Park are found in this area. Some of the gnarled oaks here could be up to 300 years old. There used to be a shelter in the Gum Slade known as the Mayors Arbour.

Opposite below: As regards the name Gum Slade it is only partly revealing. *Slade* means a valley, which would relate to the low-lying path through the Gum Slades ancient oaks. Gum is made from the sap of trees but as far as I know there are no records relating to the gum being taken from the trees in the Park.

Westwood Coppice comprises approximately forty acres of woodland. Here there are some fine Scots pines and oaks. Westwood Coppice is first mentioned in 1776. It is surrounded by a bank and ditch like the earlier coppices but unlike them it was a new plantation, so it is straight sided rather than irregular in shape.

four
The
Heathland

Aerial view of Sutton Park. Looking towards Streetly Gate, 1997.

Opposite below: Stream in Longmoor Valley. Sutton Park is special in that it has wet heath close to dry heath, close to mires, close to bogs and close to open water, which gives a fantastic variety of habitat. Man has looked after the heathland and used it to his own advantage. Heather has many uses, including thatching, track building and beer making. Bracken was often used as a winter bedding for animals. Gorse also had many uses, including fuel, broom making and winter fodder.

Above: Looking to Longmoor Pool. Heathland is classed as a distinctive habitat type, which has cultural, historic and landscape importance. It is typically found on nutrient-poor mineral soils, particularly acidic and podsols. It is often associated with heather species, course grasses, gorse and other lower plants. It is also a habitat which has largely been managed by human exploitation, for example fuel gathering, and the grazing of livestock.

Heather and gorse, The Park, Sutton Coldfield

Heather and gorse in Sutton Park. Many heathland products were eaten, including bilberries, blackberries, cranberries and crab apples. Bilberries would have been an important harvest in the past, blackberries were the number one harvest with bilberries being the second. They were used for food and for the making of dyes. During the Second World War the RAF tried to buy up the whole of the British harvest so they could dye their uniforms but they lost out to Robinsons, so instead of the bilberries being used for the dyeing of uniforms they ended up as jam.

Sutton Coldfield Park . The road to Streetley.

The road to Streetly. Some species of plants and animals adapted to these conditions and became dependant on their survival. The less fertile areas were ideal for the grazing of livestock.

Donkeys in Sutton Park. The use of grazing in Sutton Park is a long established management technique. The Park has been almost continuously grazed at low level since at least the twelfth century, when deer parks were created. The habitats of the Park have benefited from the grazing and it is mainly due to the activities of these animals that the heath and grasslands have retained their diversity.

Cattle in Sutton Park, *c.* 1945. From the late 1890s to the 1990s there has been a general decline in the amount of grazing in Sutton Park. Maps show that the spread of scrub from 1948 to 1984 and the number of cattle grazing in the Park corresponds exactly with the amount of scrub covering the Park.

Above: Longmoor Valley, *c. 1945.* Sutton Park today is grazed by a variety of animals. Rabbits graze extensively throughout the park. In the southern section cattle graze from April to October; in 1893 there were 733 head of cattle, horses and ponies grazing in the Park. Today there are approximately 125 cattle.

Left: Burnt area near to the Shooting Butts. In the northern section Exmoor ponies graze throughout the year, being introduced into the Park in 1999. These grazing animals have different effects on the heath, helping to maintain a mosaic of vegetation types and structures. In comparison to many other heathland sites in the country, Sutton Park benefits from its historic enclosures and association with its grazing animals.

five
The Pools

LONGMORE POOL, SUTTON PARK,

The Boat House on Bracebridge Pool. All of the pools in Sutton Park are man-made, dating from around 1413 to 1757. Their purpose was to provide fish for the local people of the area and to drive the water-powered mills.

Bracebridge Pool. Bracebridge Pool is of medieval origin and like the other pools in the Park, it is manmade. Its original purpose was for fish, mainly bream, which were supplied to the Lord of the Manor.

Above: Bracebridge Pool, September 1959. It is thought that the pool was constructed by Sir Ralph Bracebridge, who was ranger of the Park during the reign of Henry V (1413-1421). Leland, in the *Itinerary* (1535) says that Richard Beauchamp, Earl of Warwick, is said to have constructed five pools, all with great and costly heads of stone. Four were passed to Ralph Bracebridge in 1420. The pool took its name from him and is still used today. (Dr John Raines)

Right: Bracebridge Pool, September 1959. Pools like this were very important in that period; they were used to provide a Lenten fare in places so far from the sea that marine fish were almost unknown. Bracebridge Pool was granted to the ranger on condition that he supplied the Earls of Warwick with either £10 rent or 120 bream at 1s 8d each. Bream baked in flour and seasoned with spice, pepper, saffron, cloves and cinnamon was a favourite at that time. Just below the dam were the stews in which the fish were kept. These were covered under the surplus railway soil when the railway line was built in 1879. (Dr John Raines)

Bracebridge Pool, September 1959. Having served its purpose as a fish provider, during the sixteenth century the pool was drained and turned into 'good meadow ground'. It well may be thanks to Bishop Vesey that the pool was reinstated. The bishop had been so impressed by the prosperity the weaving trade had bought to the west of England he supplied townsmen with looms and people to instruct them in their use. Various processes were involved with weaving, one being fulling. Richard Barlow, who was a Sutton tailor, made an application to the Warden and Society to reinstate the pool at Bracebridge and construct a fulling mill. He was granted his wish on 20 August 1577. A new dam was erected, turning the pasture once more into a pool. (Dr John Raines)

Bracebridge Cottage. The pool is almost twenty-one acres in extent, and can be found in the north of Sutton Park. It is flanked by Pool Hollies Wood on one side and Darnel Hurst. Its overflow helps fill up Blackroot Pool.

Little Bracebridge Pool, September 1959. The earliest known map of Sutton Park 'A Plan and Measurement of Sutton Park Proposed by way of a Plan for Enclosing the Park, Commons and Wastes of Sutton Coldfield', (1779) shows Bracebridge Pool as one large pool. The Corn Rent Map of 1824 and the Valuation Map of Sutton Coldfield, dated 1857, also show one large pool. However, by the 1889 1st Edition Ordnance Survey map it had become the two pools. It can be presumed then that, over the years, the area between what is now the two pools became silted up. (Dr John Raines)

Fish Stews, Little Bracebridge. 1988. Little Bracebridge was also the site of fish stews, a shallow stretch of water where fish were placed for fattening.

Blackroot Pool. Until the year 1757 the valley lying between Bracebridge Pool and the pool at Park House was a boggy area with a stream running through. Plans for making a new pool were under discussion between members of the Warden and Society on 26 September 1757. They were considering a request from Nicolas Dolphin and Edward Hommer. It was agreed that Dolphin and Hommer 'shall have liberty to make a drain or pool in the valley below Black Root'. It is interesting to note that the name Black Root was in existence before the pool was created.

The most popular story as to the origin of the name is said to relate to an old oak tree, the blackened root or stump of which stood on a mound near to the centre of the pool. For many years the stump was used to tether boats, until a storm in the 1870s blew the boats to shore, dragging the stump with them.

In 1868 the pool was known as Perkins Pool (named after William Steel Perkins, who became its tenant in 1861). Swimmers' dressing rooms were erected on the dam.

Boathouses on Blackroot Pool.

Blackroot pool is renowned as a carp water, with both common and mirror carp living there.

Mʳ C TOWNSHEND'S
MOTOR LAUNCH,

Above: In 1913 the motor launch *Nancy* was a popular tourist attraction on the pool.

Opposite: Agreement between the Corporation of Sutton Coldfield and Mr C. Townsend for permission to put a motorboat on Blackroot Pool, 1908.

An Agreement made the 16th day of January 1908 Between the Mayor Aldermen and Burgesses of the Borough of Sutton Coldfield of the one part and Charles Townshend of Sutton Coldfield Caterer of the other part

Whereas the said Charles Townshend hath applied to the said Corporation for permission to place a Motor Boat on Blackroot Pool in the said Borough which the said Corporation hath agreed to grant on the conditions hereinafter appearing Now this Agreement witnesseth

1. The said permission is granted subject to the said Charles Townshend observing the following regulations

Regulations

1. The Motor Boat shall not be driven at a speed exceeding five miles per hour.

2. No Steam Whistle or other Mechanical Hooter shall be used while the boat is stationary or for any other purpose other than as a warning

Keeper's Pool. It is said that Keeper's pool was constructed by John Holte, keeper of The Chase in Henry VI's time, hence the name Keeper's Pool. It was not part of the Park. It was owned by the Holte family, which became united with the Somerville family. In 1849 there appeared a minute of the Warden and Society that 'the Pool in Sutton Park called Keeper's Pool should belong to the Corporation'. Later that year the Society were informed that Lord Somerville was open to an exchange for Keeper's Pool. However, it was not until 1879 that Keeper's Pool was purchased with the Boldmere allotment land, some nineteen acres in all, for £3,500.

Keeper's Pool looking towards the dam.

Longmoor Pool. A minute in the Warden and Society meeting in 1733 states that Mr John Riland shall have the liberty to make a dam and pool in a croft at Longmoor Brook to hold for twenty-one years at one shilling yearly. The embankment was to be fifty yards long, eleven feet high, ten yards broad at the bottom and five at the top.

In 1754, a term of twenty-one years was granted to John Riland for 'like rent and the allowance of a dish of fish for the warden for the time being at every general fishing of the pool'.

POWELLS POOL SUTTON PARK

BOATING ! FISHING ! REFRESHMENTS !

POWELL'S POOL,
SUTTON PARK.

This magnificent sheet of water is by far the Largest and Best Boating and Fishing Pool in the district.

STEAM, SAILING, AND ROWING BOATS.

THE FINE NEW STEAMBOAT "FOAM,"
(WITH BOARD OF TRADE CERTIFICATE,)

Will make frequent trips round the lake every fine afternoon during the season.

The Pool is well stocked with Fish. Day Tickets are issued.

It is close to the Boldmere entrance to the Park ; the way from the Sutton entrance is to the left, past the Crystal Palace and the entrance to Windley Pool, and up the carriage drive between the Donkey Course and the tea tables—on turning to the left at the top, the Pool will be seen.

Teas and Refreshments of best quality at moderate charges.
Schools and large Parties specially arranged for.

H. A. DONE. Lessee.

Above: Powell's Pool. Until the year 1730 water rising in the Longmoor Valley ran unimpeded into Wyndley Pool. There were no dams at either Longmoor or Powell's at that time. The forty-eight acres of land now covered by the waters of Powell's pool were part of the Holtes Estates. The dam was erected by Thomas Holte in 1730.

Left: In 1904 the Boldmere Swimming Club used the pool for their morning swim. The Pool was also popular for trips on the steam boat *Foam*, sailing and rowing. Today the pool is used by the sea cadets and for sailing.

Opposite below: Wyndley Pool. The construction of five pools, all with 'great and costly heads of stone', and attributed to the Earl of Warwick during the reign of Henry V is the first indication as to the possible originator and creation of Wyndley Pool. Wyndley Pool was the first to have a dam erected to hold the waters rising in Longmoor Valley. Powell's and Longmoor dams were built considerably later in 1733, so it appears that Wyndley is in fact the oldest pool.

The Pool did not come into the possession of the Corporation until 1937. The white house in the middle of this photograph was the first home of the Sutton Coldfield Sea Cadet Corp before they moved to the Training Ship Sutton Coldfield, which is just outside of the Park besides the Park Keeper's Lodge.

WYNDLEY POOL, SUTTON PARK, SUTTON COLDFIELD.   H.1500

When Leland, the King's Antiquary, visited Sutton Coldfield in around 1535 he recorded the fact that Wyndley Pool was in existence. He referred to the pool by the name Wyndle. Wyndley Pool was one of a number of pools that were drained in the 1500s, along with Mill Pool, Cross Pool, Keeper's and Bracebridge Pools.

Wyndley Pool from the Driffold. The pool did not become part of the Park until 1937, with Powell's Pool and other lands. At the time of the depression at the end of the 1920s Sutton Corporation decided to construct Monmouth Drive with the aid of a grant from the Unemployment Grants Committee, the intention being to provide work for the unemployed and to create rateable value on undeveloped land. Agreements were entered into with the owners of the land through which the new road was to run. The 25,091 acres owned by The National Children's Home was conveyed to the Corporation on 25 April 1935 and the remainder of the land owned by the Trustees of the Somerville Estates on 16 March 1937. The Conveyance from the Sommerville Trustees contained a covenant by the Corporation to use the land on the north side of the new road (Monmouth Drive) only as forming an addition to Sutton Park. The trustees, at the same time, declared in a separate document that this covenant should not prevent the playing of open-air games on the said land and the erection of suitable buildings in connection with the games. The total area transferred to the Corporation was 152 acres.

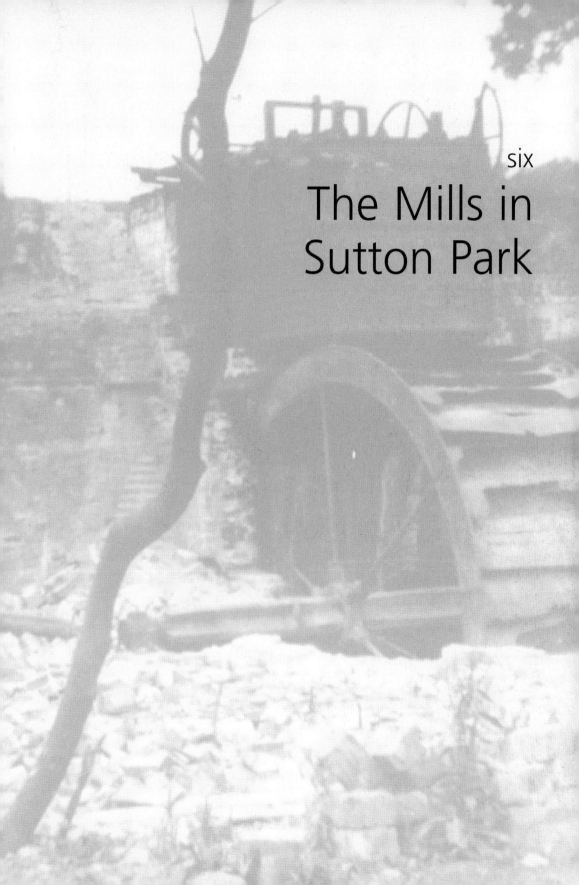

six

The Mills in
Sutton Park

Blackroot Dam. Sutton Park's 2,400 acres collects vast quantities of water, and its soil, consisting mainly of sandy silts and conglomerate,s quickly releases this water from two small streams, one near to Bracebridge in the north of the Park, the other at Longmoor valley in the south-west. Seven dams created pools within Sutton Park, six of which at some time worked watermills. Keeper's Pool is the only pool not to have worked a mill.

Blackroot Mill. In 1759 Joseph Duncumb joined a partnership with Nicholas Dolphin and Edward Homer and the three obtained permission to erect '… one waterwheel for a mill for dressing leather, commonly called a leather mill, and to make a cut or channel from the said pool (Blackroot) into the common watercourse from the said wheel in such a manner as they think proper'. If the mill was ever built it was not on the dam itself, but near to the end of the dam where the gravel pit and saw mill are situated today. It is thought that this was where limepits were made. The animal skins would have been soaked in the limepits to remove any hair or flesh prior to the tanning process in the mill. The skins were then placed in large revolving drums containing the tanning liquor. It was these drums which would have been turned by the waterwheel. The skins were then removed and dried, stretched, smoothed, dyed and given a grain. The mill and waterwheel would have probably have been made of wood taken from the Park, and the interior of the mill would have been dark, smelly and noisy.

There are no photographs of the leather mill, nor a date when this building was either built or pulled down, but in the gravel pit, where the limepits may have been, there is now a sawmill. By 1895 a steam engine was being used to work a stonebreaker, replaced by a turbine which was powered by the water from the pool. Gravel was also being taken from the Park's pits. This was either sold or used to repair the roads in the Park. A sawmill also existed, as whenever trees were felled in Sutton Park, some of this timber would be taken to Blackroot Gravel Pit to the sawmill for conversion into fencing. During the Second World War the gravel pit played its part in the war effort, for in 1943 permission was granted to the Civil Defence to construct a rifle range there. The same year saw repairs to the saw bearings. The sawmill would by now have been powered by electricity. Today the pits at Blackroot are still used as a sawmill.

Bracebridge Dam. Bracebridge Mill and Pool owes its existence to Richard Barlow, a Sutton tailor who in 1577 was granted permission by Sutton Corporation to dig up a meadow, rebuild the dam and recreate the pool, which had been drained in the sixteenth century. He was allowed to build a fulling mill, which was powered by water from the pool. It is likely that this mill was built of wood and would have been a single-storey building.

Inside the mill fulling stocks, large wooden hammers, would pound the cloth in wooden water tubs, thus shrinking it and making it more durable. Urine was used in those days to cleanse the cloth of grease, so the inside of the mill would be somewhat smelly. It was usual to pay local people a penny for a large potfull. After the cleansing and fulling process had been completed the cloth would have been spread out in an area close to the mill and held off the ground by tenterhooks to dry. The mill did not have a very long life. The last record of it is in 1588 when Humphrey Kene conveyed two fulling mills to Simon Perott. The mill would have been situated about where the restaurant The Boat House is situated today. This is where the water leaves the pool and where the waterwheel would probably been situated.

Longmoor Mill Sales Advertisement, 1824. Longmoor Mill, a corn mill, is one of the few mills for which there is a construction and demolition date. Situated just inside of the Park, about 440 yards from the Banners Gate entrance, it was built in 1754. Richard Reynolds, a wheelwright, borrowed £60 to pay for the construction. Rent for the mill was forty shillings per annum. After three years he was unable to make a proper living from it so he applied for permission to build a lean-to or shed for dressing leather. He would have installed a large wooden revolving drum in which he cured the leather, soaking it in tannin. This was not a success either, and in 1762 the mill was using the drums for polishing buttons for the Birmingham button trade.

The mill was built of brick and its breast-shot waterwheel stood outside. In 1823 the mill was rebuilt at a cost of £700 because it was in such a bad condition. In 1832 an inspection of the mill revealed the waterwheel was badly damaged and the wheel working the dressing machine not in a proper state. The miller Mr Dutton was ordered to put it back into working order. From 1850 on there followed a succession of millers unable to make a success of it. The wheel was again replaced in 1851 at a cost of £198 16s. The years 1877 and 1878 saw further repairs and improvements to the mill.

BOLDMERE, ENTRANCE AND OLD MILL.

In 1750 William Powell was working the mill as a forge, and in the 1830s Francis Parker was making spades and various edged tools there which were exported to every country in the Commonwealth. Spade Mill, as it was known in 1855, employed thirty men and boys to work the tilt hammer and grindstones.

Opposite above: By the early 1900s the mill cottage was tenanted, but the mill was no longer working. Its occupiers were selling refreshments and teas to Park visitors. In 1938 the derelict mill was demolished and today only the dam and the pool remain.

Opposite below: Powell's Pool, Spade Mill, 1900. The earliest record of a mill at Powell's Pool is in the year 1733, when John Wyatt erected a mill and set up an experimental cotton-spinning machine, and there spun the first ever thread of cotton ever produced by mechanical means. He did this some sixty years before Richard Arkwright became famous for his Spinning Jenny. Wyatt's machine was only about two feet square. Unfortunately due to lack of funds he failed to patent his rollers. His partner Lewis Paul took over Wyatt's invention and Arkwright's successful Spinning Jenny in 1769 incorporated Wyatt's rollers. Wyatt died a pauper while the hank of cotton is preserved in the Birmingham Museum.

Left: Pitch Back Waterwheel at Spade Mill, 1936. During the 1820s the mill also became a rolling mill, rolling steel for use as nibs by the Birmingham pen trade. In the Second World War, John E. Mappelbeck produced brass strips for the war effort at the mill. These strips were for the making of bullets. At the end of the war production ceased at the mill, and gradually the empty building fell into decay. It was demolished in 1936.

Below: All that remains of the mill today are the millstone steps, which lead into Powell's Pool.

Opposite above: Park House before alterations. Park House Blade Mill was situated in a private enclosure within the Park. The outbuildings today are used as a restaurant but in the days of Elizabeth I the mill was Sutton Coldfield's first blade mill and the first mill to employ a tilt hammer which was used to shape metal into blades. This mill, occupied by John Hayberd and owned by Johanne Whately, widow of Northfield, Nicholas Reynolds of Kings Norton and Humphrey Bradley of Higgeley, sold in 1597 for £40. In 1624, it was sold by Thomas and William Stanton, this time for £50. The new owner Walter Payton owned the mill for fifty-four years, but during that time allowed all work to cease and by 1678 the mill buildings had been demolished.

Looking up the lower field, the rising ground gives the appearance of possibly having been a dam. Shortly after Thomas Addyes of Maney took over Park House he rebuilt the blade mill and installed a tilt hammer in around 1700, so the sound of the thump of the tilt was resounding around the district once more. The top field in the enclosure was turned into a millpond by erecting a dam across the field, with a small millrace leading down the side. Waters from Keeper's and Blackroot pools fed into this pool. Today it is silted up and is meadow again, but the ancient dam can still be discerned. By the year 1811 the mill was occupied by George Brown, and his mill-plated saws, spade and shovels. It also ground saws and files and employed many people. This mill and pool can be seen on Sutton Coldfield Library's earliest known map of Sutton Park, 'A Plan and Admeasurement of Sutton Park', dated 1779. The pool had silted up by the mid-1800s. From 1851 John and Harriet Wiggen of Birmingham were to occupy the Park House property, but by then the mill had been demolished.

Park House after alterations. In 1898 the cottages where the mill owners lived were considerably altered. The front of the larger buildings were extended and black and white timbers added to castellated extensions at each end, leaving only a small part of the middle and end buildings unaltered. The hill outside the grounds, known as Blade Mill Hill, was used for a bonfire to celebrate the Coronation of George V on 22 June 1911. In 1922 Mr F. Lonsdale Allen, chairman of Gill & Russell Ltd, tube makers of Walsall, moved into Park House as tenant, paying his three sisters who had inherited the property. In 1948 Sutton Coldfield Corporation purchased the property for £19,250, which consisted of ten acres including pools and woods. Since the death of Mr Lonsdale Allen in 1954, the property has been used as a restaurant.

Wyndley Pool and Mill. It is unlikely that it was made to support a watermill, but more as a source of fish for the occupiers of the Manor House. Wyndley was one of a number of pools that were drained in the 1500s. 'By the mid-sixteenth century four pools in the manor had been drained and turned into good meadow ground. These pools had been known as Mill Pool, Cross Pool, Wyndle Pool, Keepers Pool and Bracebridge.' By 1576 three watermills were conveyed with the Manor House, one of which was probably Wyndley. The earliest confirmation of this mill is in 1669, when an entry in the Parish Registers of Holy Trinity Church records the death of John Wood of 'Bladd Mill' on 24 December.

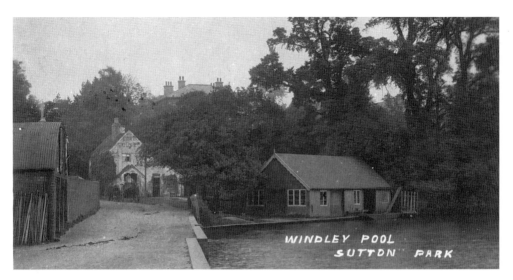

Conditions in a blade mill were very unhealthy, with dust from the grindstones filling the air and damaging the lungs of the workers – there were no extractor fans then. Consequently the parish records record the deaths of several young men in their twenties from the mill. The approach to the mill was by way of Wyndley Lane, one of the oldest thoroughfares in Sutton, and until 1827 was the only access for traffic into the park with the road passing over the dam. In 1778 the mill possessed two waterwheels, one of them worked as a forge for metalware by Thomas Parkes. A high watermark was fixed to a stone facing the dam so that each mill should receive its proper share of water. By 1840 the mill had been converted into a sawmill and when the Birmingham to Sutton railway was under construction, thousands of wheelbarrows made at the mill were used by the construction workers.

The sluice gates at Wyndley Pool. On 19 June 1901 the dam collapsed, carrying away the waterwheel which was located at the side of the mill. Mr Thickbroom, the tenant, was on the dam when it collapsed but escaped injury. Both the dam and wheel were restored to working order. Photographs taken around 1910 show tree trunks waiting to be sawn up. Mr Thickbroom appears to be the last working miller at Wyndley.

Logs outside Wyndley Mill. In 1937 Wyndley Pool was taken over by Sutton Coldfield Corporation and so became part of the Park. By this time the work at the mill had ceased and the building was beginning to decay. The length of the building was the correct length for an indoor rifle range and for a while was the home for a rifle club who set up a rifle range inside. In 1961 the roof of the derelict mill collapsed under the weight of snow, and shortly after the mill was demolished.

seven

Military Use

Protection Trench. Each year in the 1870s the Old Militia used to march from Thorpe Street Barracks in Birmingham to Sutton Park to camp for fourteen days and practice rifle shooting in the area between Westwood Coppice and Rowton Hill. The most conspicuous feature of the old range still remaining is the Target Butt at the Rowton Hill end of Donegal's ride, where the artificial mound conceals the trench constructed within it for the protection of the men who changed the targets above them. The six-inch Ordnance Survey map of 1884 shows the butts, flagpole and target, and the positions for firing at if from distances for 200, 300 500, 600, 800, 900 or 1,000 yards, from the direction of the present Banners Gate toilets. By 1902, according to the OS, the range had been abandoned and no trace of the firing position remained.

Targets and Practice Trench. There is, however, evidence still to be found of the military camp, and careful searching beneath the long grass and overgrown gorse in the vicinity of the old 800 yards firing position will reveal the circular drainage trench some nine inches deep and eight inches wide which had been all round the perimeters of at least ten army bell tents. Some of the circles are about fifteen to seventeen feet in diameter.

The wood inside the Park from Streetly Gate. It was here, on the right of the road from the gate, that the Militia of the 1880s set up camp. In the late 1800s voluntary service in the army was very popular. The Birmingham Regiment usually had about 750 at camp in Sutton Park.

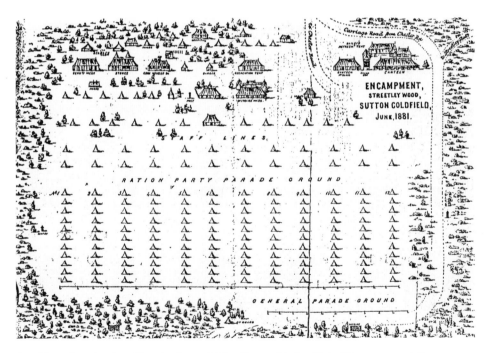

ENCAMPMENT,
STREETLEY WOOD,
SUTTON COLDFIELD,
JUNE, 1881.

A guide written by the officer in charge, Major Gem, with Sgt Major Thompson and Quarter Master Griffiths in support, gives us the following information: Reveille at 5 a.m; Drill 6-7.30 a.m; Breakfast 8 a.m – ½lb bread, ¼lb ham; 1 pint coffee; Morning Parade 10.30 a.m; Drill to 12.30 p.m; Dinner 1.30 p.m – 1lb meat, ¼lb bread, 1lb pots; Drill to 3.30 p.m; Tea and free from 6 p.m. Tea consisted of one pint tea, ½lb bread, 1oz butter or 2oz cheese.

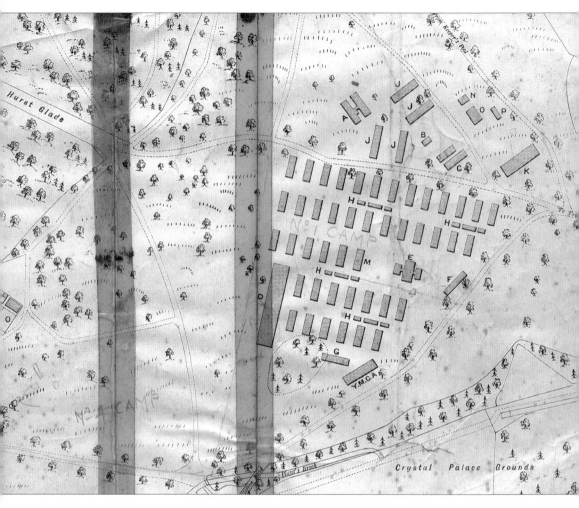

At the beginning of the First World War men from the Birmingham PALS 1st and 2nd Battalion were in training in the Park. The newly formed battalions of the 1st and 2nd left New Street Station on 5 October and 12 October 1914. The 1st Battalion camped near to the Crystal Palace site. Both battalions moved into their newly completed huts during the second week of April in 1915. This map shows the layout of Camp 1 the 1st Battalion, near to the Crystal Palace grounds.

Opposite above: The forty huts measured sixty feet by twenty feet. The camp was taken over by the Reserve Battalion of the Royal Warwickshire when the 1st and 2nd Battalions left on 25/26 June 1915. This map shows the layout of Camp 2, the 2nd Battalion, near Powell's Pool.

Opposite below: Men of the 2nd Battalion cleaning out the new huts prior to occupation in August 1915. At first the PALS recruits were billeted out with families in the royal town, but at the beginning of 1915 wooden huts were provided.

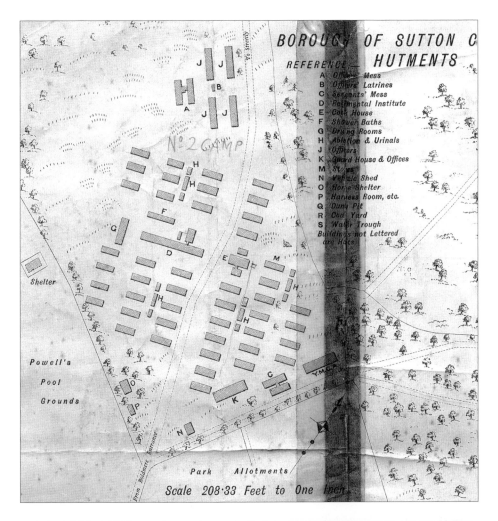

BOROUGH OF SUTTON C
HUTMENTS

REFERENCE.—

A Officers' Mess
B Officers' Latrines
C Sergeants' Mess
D Regimental Institute
E Cook House
F Shower Baths
G Drying Rooms
H Ablution & Urinals
J Officers
K Guard House & Offices
M Stores
N Vehicle Shed
O Horse Shelter
P Harness Room, etc.
Q Dung Pit
R Coal Yard
S Water Trough
Buildings not Lettered
are Huts

Nº 2 CAMP

Shelter

Powell's
Pool
Grounds

Park   Allotments

Scale 208·33 Feet to One Inch.

Volunteers in late 1914, showing off their new uniforms. The 2 Platoon A Company are situated near Powell's Pool. A manuscript note on the reverse of this postcard states that 'everyone had been killed or wounded between 15 September 1915 and 1918'.

The area near Town Gate was used for two searchlights ('anti-aircraft projector lights') placed in the Park during the Second World War. A number of bombs were dropped near this unit, causing at least one death.

Just as in the First World War there was a camp near Westwood Coppice holding German and Italian prisoners of war. Originally used for civilian internees for three weeks, it was also used for Czech soldiers. A report in the *Birmingham Dispatch* dated 15 August 1941 stated that the German and Austrian internees were complaining of being pestered by mosquitoes. The ground was also said to be 'waterlogged'. Questions were raised in the House of Commons in which it was suggested that 'inadequate preparations' had been made for the reception of the men. There were about 700 aliens in the camp, having been transferred from Kempton Park some two weeks earlier. The internees lived in tents, enclosed by double high-wire fencing which stretched a considerable distance beyond the confines of the camp. The internees complained that the camp was not suitable for elderly people. They were mostly between forty-five and seventy years of age. The camp was used until October 1945 and dismantling commenced in January 1946.

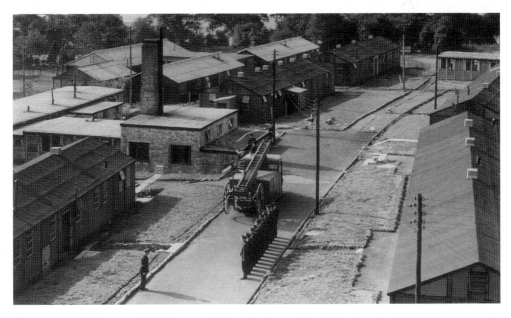

The Ministry of Works and Buildings requisitioned land near Powell's Pool and a Civil Defence camp for the Mobile Reserve was erected. It was taken over as a training centre by the National Fire Service.

Sutton Coldfield Park. On the road to Streetley. Looking towards Keepers Pool. [illegible] Photo Copyright

It is hard to believe that the land directly ahead from this view, (looking towards Queens Coppice) was used during the Second World War for testing military vehicles such as Sherman Tanks. It was necessary to make a new entrance at Banners Gate to give access to the large tanks. The last tank was tested in December 1945. The ground had been in continuous use from September 1940, and became a hideous mess, yet the Park has regenerated well from the tracks of the tanks.

The gun site at Streetly was used by both the American and British forces, but according to a Parks and Estates Committee Report the guns were never fired. Also at Streetly the Warwickshire War Agricultural Executive Committee requisitioned some ninety-four acres of ground for the growing of vegetables. It is known that there was an anti-aircraft gun unit during the Second World War, situated near the Four Oaks Gate. There are no known photographs and there is very little information on this. Can any of our readers help? Displaced persons from Europe came to Sutton Coldfield. It is said that a camp for some of them was sited south of Holly Hurst. Any information on this camp would be appreciated.

BERTRAM Mills Circus

eight

Leisure,
Recreation
and Sport

Staffordshire Beagles in Sutton Park, 17 March 1954. A deed dated 1775 records a meeting of certain local gentry at the Red Lion on the High Street, Sutton Coldfield, when the Rt Hon. Lord Spencer Hamilton, acting under the authority of his father, the Earl of Donegal, agreed to hunt in Sutton Park. Part of the terms of the agreement was, that the 'horses, hounds and servants should lie in Sutton every night before the hunt, and that notice of the time and place of throwing off should be left in writing at George Sicknell's at Salford Bridge, Canwell Gate and the kennels at Sutton, and further agreed that the hounds shall draw until three o'clock each day in the case of not finding before'.

Above: Joint Meet of the Staffordshire Beagles and Warwickshire Beagles, Sutton Park, 18 March 1959. Hunting was not new to Sutton Park. The 1528 Charter gave Warden and Society and the male inhabitants of the town, manor and lordship and their successors the right of hunting, fishing and fowling in the Park, but with the condition that a licence from the Warden and Society had to be obtained. (Dr John Raines)

Right: Sutton Park was part of the Staffordshire Beagles' territory. The Warwickshire Beagles, who were based right in the south of the county, were the visitors. The Staffordshire huntsmen wore bright blue coats and their Warwickshire counterparts maroon ones. (Dr John Raines)

Opposite below: Staffordshire Beagles, Sutton Park, 17 March 1954. The Earl of Donegal, who lived at Fisherwick Hall near Lichfield, is remembered today with Donegal Road, which runs between Chester Road and Queslett Road and the path in Sutton Park, which runs from the Royal Oak gate to the top of Rowton's Hill. In 1775 there were seven packs hunting in the Park, including the South Staffordshire Hunt.

The racecourse near Holly Knoll. Although horse racing had been held in Sutton Park before 1844, the first properly organised racecourse in Sutton Park was located to the north side of Holly Knoll, the present-day railway and Blackroot Pool. Although all traces of the course have long gone, part of the course can be traced where it curves in a wide sweep up to the plateau to the end of Blackroot Pool, and through a cutting in part of Holly Knoll. Costing £1,000 to build, the inaugural meeting took place on 19 and 20 June 1844. The main event of the meeting was the Wyndley Pool Handicap Stakes. The course, an oblong and a straight run in, held the Birmingham Stakes in 1847. The spectator banks can just be made out today.

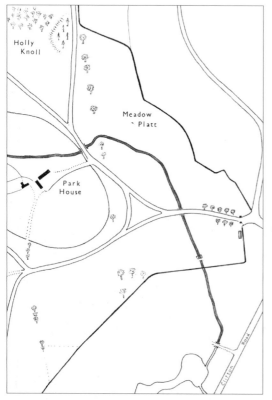

A second and much larger racecourse was constructed near Westwood Coppice in 1868. The course, on an elongated oval, covered just over a mile-and-three-quarters in length with the straight seven furlongs. The inaugural meeting took place on 9 and 10 July 1868. Special trains were put on from New Street Station to enable the race-goers to get to the races and watch from the grandstand, which held over 500 people. This course ran its last race in 1879. In 1973 local man Bob Burns proposed that a racecourse be built in Longmoor Valley with grandstands and all the facilities of a modern racecourse. His proposals were not accepted by the Council.

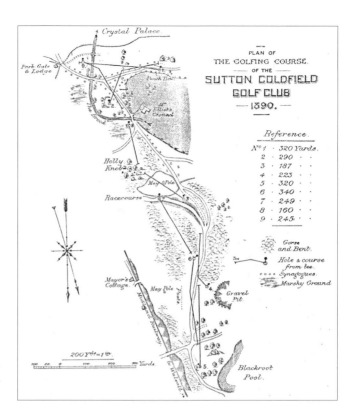

Plan of the Golf Course 1890. The rector of Sutton Coldfield, the Revd W.K. Riland Bedford, introduced golf into the Park around 1880. The first nine-hole golf course was constructed near to Meadow Platt.

Some of the greens and bunkers can still be seen today. The bunker to the first green can be seen in the form of a hollow near the hedge in front of Park House.

Above: Aerial view of Sutton Park, showing the eighteen-hole golf course. The course, on the Streetly side, was established in 1889 when the Sutton Coldfield Golf Club was formed. A rulebook for the club in 1889 gives fifty-four rules and eight local rules.

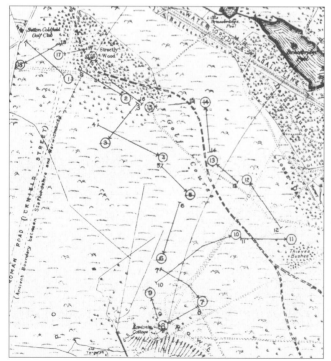

Left: Map showing the course of the Sutton Coldfield Golf Club. The first course was only nine holes but by June 1893 it became necessary to extend the course to eighteen holes to meet popular demand.

The Clubhouse, *c.* 1914. The clubhouse was built in 1897 for £1,350 and the first corrugated club house which had stood on the same site was sold to the Burton-on-Trent Golf Club for £50. An extension to the dressing room was put on in 1904 and in 1909 the lounge was extended. On 3 September 1908 fire destroyed part of the building and in 1961 the balcony had to be removed for safety reasons.

Above: Approach to the first tee.

Above: Rowton's Well, 1846. Rowton's Well is one of three wells in Sutton Park fed by natural spring waters. It is difficult to date the construction of the wells. According to an anonymous writer in 1762, this well, north of Longmoor Pool, was famous for curing 'inveterate, cutaneous and chronic ailments' that baffled physicians.

Left: It was said that people living in the mining districts around Walsall would come to drink water from the well and to bathe in the water. In Victorian times mixed bathing was not allowed, so a flag would be hoisted when the ladies were bathing. The Birmingham Eye Hospital used the waters from this well until the 1930s because of its medicinal properties.

Right: Rowton's Well, 1900. Harry
H. Horton, writing of the well in his
poem on Sutton Park in 1844, says:

Whose water yields, in a dark
    affliction's hour,
A balmy hope, a health restoring
    power:
There pale consumption from its
    crystal bed
Walks with new vigour and tread.
While infants, plunged within its
    cold embrace,
Grow strong with time and from a
    manly race
E'en now I love to seek thy
    wholesome spell
And plunge within the far famed
    'Rowton Well.'

Druids Well. In 1813 Sutton Coldfield Corporation proposed that the pits and springs in Sutton Park should be put to public use. In 1815 wells were made at the springs at Pool Hollis Wood, Druids Well, and at Keeper's Pool. Vandals reduced Druids Well to a pile of rubble in 1982. In 1986 The Friends of Sutton Park made an appeal to save the well when the Sutton Park's Advisory Committee recommended that the well be sealed and capped. The well was not sealed nor capped but the cost of rebuilding the well proved to be too prohibitive. Sometime in the 1990s the well was rebuilt by an unknown person, but unfortunately it has been destroyed yet again.

Keeper's Well was capped with a huge concrete block for many years, but now the well can be seen as it should be. Note how open the view is. Today Keeper's Pool cannot be seen from the well because of the trees.

Keeper's Pool and Keeper's Baths. In 1864 the General Purposes of the Corporation requested that the Parks Committee enquire as to the expense of making a swimming bath in the Park and to the locality they recommended. In March 1868 it was suggested that Perkin's Pool be made available in lieu of making a new pool by erecting a small shed and landing space. In 1874 there was another suggestion that a public swimming bath in the Park should be constructed below Blackroot Pool. However, the Corporation replied that although it was desirable to construct such a bath, 'it was not advisable in the present financial state of the corporate funds to incur such an expense at the present time'.

On 6 April 1887 Sutton Corporation finally decided that the swimming baths should be built, provided the cost was no more than £200. On 30 July the baths were opened. Bathing took place behind unroofed wooden walls, for the sake of Victorian modesty. There is a tale that the interior walls were painted black to make it less easy to see the human form.

Keeper's Baths, 1951. By the 1900s the swimming baths had been extended, but the first major reconstruction was not until the 1930s, when the baths were opened up for all to watch from Keeper's Pool. Cubicles similar to beach huts were added at this time.

By the 1950s people were swimming in Keeper's Pool as well as the swimming baths.

The site became so popular that in the 1960s the building was rebuilt.

The swimming baths were destroyed by vandals in March 2003. The Council proposed a state-of-the-art lido, sports complex and education centre be built near to Powell's Pool. However, strong public opinion saw that idea shelved. Instead, the Clifton Road Youth Centre has been improved and extended.

Rowing and paddle boats on Blackroot Pool. Boating on the pools in the Park had been a popular pastime.

Since Victorian times *Crusader* was a popular boat on Blackroot Pool. It was rumored that this 1930s little thirty-foot motorboat carried troops at Dunkirk during the Second World War. In 1984 a ride on the boat would have cost 50p for adults and 25p for children. (Bernard R. Haynes)

Left: Train trips to Sutton Park were very popular. The coming of the railway, which opened in June 1862, brought a sharp increase in the number of visitors to the Park. Even in the winter the railway advertised a Christmas trip to Sutton Coldfield in 1870 for skating on Wyndley Pool. The train left New Street at 12 noon and 2 p.m. and the return fare was 9d. An advertisement dated July 1911. (Dr John Raines)

SUTTON PARK.

Boating and Fishing on the Pools.
MOTOR LAUNCH ON BLACKROOT POOL.

On TUESDAY & WEDNESDAY, August 8 & 9,

Cheap Excursions

WILL BE RUN AS UNDER TO

SUTTON COLDFIELD

FROM	Times of Starting								RETURN FARES—3rd Class only			
									Tuesday, August 8.		Wednesday, August 9.	
									ADULTS.	Children over 3 and under 12 Years of Age.	ADULTS.	Children over 3 and under 12 Years of Age.
	a.m.	a.m.	p.m.	p.m.	p.m.	p.m.	p.m.					
Monument Lane	10 15	11 53	12 40	1 38	2 40	3 40	4 50		1/-	6d.	10d.	6d.
Birmingham (New Street)	10 40	12 30	1 5	2 10	3 5	4 10	5 20		10d.	5d.	9d.	4½d.
Vauxhall	10 44	12 39	1 10	2 15	3 10	4 19	5 24		9d.	4½d.	8d.	4d.
Aston	10 50	12 42	1 14	2 18	3 15	4 22	5 27		8d.	4d.	7d.	3½d.

RETURN ARRANGEMENTS.—Passengers return on day of issue only by trains leaving Sutton Coldfield at 5.0; 5.40; 6*5; 6.25; 7.0; 7.35; 8.20; 9.40; 10.10 p.m. * Not for Aston and Vauxhall.

For Excursion Bookings from Vauxhall and Aston on Bank Holiday see other bills.

Children under Three years of age free ; above Three and under Twelve Half-fares. No Luggage allowed.

Tickets can be obtained in Birmingham at the following Excursion Offices :—
Stephenson Place, 46, Snow Hill.
Swan Office, 137, New Street. 1, George Street, Parade.
Bridge Booking Office, New Street Station. 44, Hall Street.
and at the Stations.

Passengers may also obtain Tickets and Small Bills from Mr. J. W. LAZENBY, L. & N. W. Railway Excursion Agent, at :—
73, High Street, West Bromwich, Telephone No. 381.
Villa Cross, Handsworth, Telephone No. 287—Northern—Birmingham.
Small Bills can also be obtained at any of the Stations, and Company's Parcels Receiving Offices.

Persons wishing to arrange for accommodation for School, Pleasure Parties, or large Excursion Parties can do so on application to Mr. R. T. MORCOM, District Superintendent, New Street Station, Birmingham.

CONDITIONS OF ISSUE OF TICKETS.
EXCURSION TICKETS are not transferable and will be available only to and from the Stations named upon them, and any Passenger using them, on the Outward or Return Journey, at any Station short of, or beyond the Stations named upon them, or on any other date, or by any other train than mentioned on the Excursion bills, will forfeit the Ticket, and be charged the Ordinary Fare.

The Company give notice that tickets for these Excursions are issued at a reduced rate, and subject to the condition that the Company shall not be liable for any loss, damage, injury, or delay, to passengers, arising from any cause whatsoever.

The Company cannot, in any way, be responsible for detention on the line; at the same time, every exertion will be made to ensure punctuality.

All information regarding Excursion Trains on the L. & N. W. Railway, can be obtained on application to Mr. R. T. MORCOM, District Superintendent, New Street Station, Birmingham.

Euston Station, London. FRANK REE, General Manager.
July, 1911.

McCorquodale & Co. Limited, Printers, London—Works Newton—1948

Water has always attracted people in the hot weather, and here people of all ages are seen paddling in Blackroot Pool in the 1930s.

In 1893 Mr Pentland set up the Royal Robins organization to give children from the inner city of Birmingham a fun day out in the country. Many of these children had never seen a garden, let alone green fields or a large open space like Sutton Park. Special trains took the children to Sutton Coldfield Station. On arrival at Town Gate they would be given a bag of food for lunch, which included a buttered roll, a baker's bun and a piece of cake, as well as ginger beer.

Tea was between 4 p.m. and 5 p.m., which included a cup of ice cream. After a variety of organized games they gathered together around 7 p.m. for the return journey to Birmingham. It is hard to believe today, but many of the youngsters were afraid of Sutton Park because it was so green and open. It certainly looks as though these robins have had a good time.

The paddling pool near to Town Gate had always been a popular venue for people to damp their feet. However over the years the stream was misused, trends changed and the blue-tiled area looked out of character with the more modern-day thinking of the natural look of Sutton Park. It was also expensive to maintain to modern-day standards and it fell short on health and safety issues. In the 1990s it was reverted to its natural appearance.

Sutton Coldfield Winter Swimming Club, April 1929. The club was formed in September 1899 by members of the Boldmere Swimming Club. As the changing rooms at Powell's Pool were closed for the winter, it was decided to continue Sunday morning swimming through the winter at Blackroot Pool. When the club originally formed there were two rules: the annual subscription was a shilling and as nude bathing was normal at that time, anyone caught wearing a costume was fined one shilling. The first Christmas Day race was held in 1900.

Boldmere Winter Swimming, 1969. In more recent years the Christmas Day meeting started around 10 a.m. Rum and coffee and the joining of hands of all those present round the brazier was followed by the presentation of the trophies. The rum was particularly appreciated when they had finished their swim, as frequently ice had to be broken for the swim to take place. Regular club members swam every day around 7.15 a.m.

Alderman Pearson unveiling the Boldmere Swimming Club war memorial near to Powell's pool in 1921. The club had been founded in 1899 and by 1905 had nearly 400 members. The First World War resulted in many of the younger members losing their lives. After the war club members, family and friends provided a small statue as a memorial to their members. The statue can now be seen in Wyndley baths.

Skaters in 1919. For those not brave enough to swim in the pools during the winter months skating on the frozen pools was another option.

Maypole dancing. Many visitors to the Park come to watch events take place throughout the year or just to take in the scenery and enjoy refreshments.

HOLLY HURST,
—OR—
WHITE HOUSE,
SUTTON PARK.

In the Wood, near Windley Pool.

—ESTABLISHED 30 YEARS.—

VISITORS WILL BE SERVED WELL.

DINNERS, TEAS,

— * AND OTHER * —

REFRESHMENTS,

OF THE BEST QUALITY, AT MODERATE PRICES.

SCHOOLS AND LARGE PARTIES SPECIALLY CATERED FOR
AT SPECIAL PRICES.

GOOD SHELTER AND ACCOMMODATION FOR 1000 PERSONS.

PROPRIETOR, CHAS. TOWNSHEND.

TENTS FOR HIRE.   GOOD STABLING.

Above: Holly Hurst Tea Rooms. An advertisement in *Sidwell and Durant's Popular Guide to Sutton and Park* in 1890 quotes 'Charles Townsend, Refreshment Contractors, dinners, teas and refreshments of the best quality at the most moderate prices. Best accommodation in Sutton Park for schools and large parties. Good shelter for 1,000 people'.

Left: Advertisement for the Holly Hurst Tea Rooms 1890.

Park House Restaurant

A old-world house with a modern atmosphere

OPEN from 10 a.m. for

MORNING COFFEE . LUNCHEONS
TEAS, etc.

Beautifully situated in own grounds inside the Park near the main gate.   Large and small rooms available for Wedding Receptions, Whist Drives, etc.

Private Car Park   Large Tea Lawn
Tennis and Clock Golf

Powells Pool Pavilion

The largest Cafe in the Park, inside Boldmere Gate

OPEN from 10 a.m. for

**Morning Coffee, Lunches and Teas
Jugs of Tea for outside use**

SEATING FOR 350

*Ideal for Sunday School or Club Outings
also available for Dances or Whist Drives.*

**We take a Special Pride in Prompt Service and
Attention to all our Customers.**

Right: Advertisement from the *Sutton Coldfield Official Guide* for Park House Restaurant and the Powell's Pool Pavilion.

Below: The terrace at Powell's Pool Café. The *1950 Guide to Sutton Coldfield* states that the café, during the summer months, is open for breakfasts, lunches, teas, suppers and, in the winter months, midday meals are always served. Parties are catered for and the pavilion may be hired for dances, whist drives, concerts, etc. Particulars of charges may be obtained from the Borough Surveyor, Council House.

WYNDLEY POOL CAFE

Luncheons Daily — 12.30 — 2.0 p.m.
Large and small parties catered for.
Club Dinners, Wedding Receptions, Socials, etc.
Sunday School parties specially catered for.
OPEN ALL THE YEAR ROUND.
Large Table Tennis Room available in the winter season
for hire to Clubs and for weekend players.

Props.   Mr. A. H. ADDERLEY,   Mrs. E. L. WELLSBURY.

Entrance off Clifton Road.
Free Car Park for Coaches, Cars, etc.

Telephone SUTTON 6034.
WYNDLEY POOL CAFE, WYNDLEY LANE,
SUTTON PARK, SUTTON COLDFIELD

Left: Advertisement for Wyndley Café.

Opposite above: The Crystal Palace. In 1868 Mr Joe Cole, a market gardener from Perry Barr, opened the Royal Promenade Gardens on a thirty-acre site between the town and the Park. In February 1878 an article in the *Sutton Coldfield News* gave the following information: 'Sutton Coldfield is shortly to be provided with an additional attraction in the form of a building comprising an hotel, a winter garden, a skating rink and an aquarium. The hotel building, with façade overlooking the Park, will be executed in red brick with Bath stone dressings and ornamental towers, covered, like the roof of the hotel, with slates. At the rear of this will be a large winter garden, fitted up with an orchestra; and, while during the whole of the year there will be a display of flowers and plants here, the place will be available for concerts, public dinners, balls, flower shows, and similar purposes ...'

Blackroot Refreshment Rooms

EST. 65 YEARS.   Proprietress : E. M. TOWNSHEND.

WHEN in Sutton Park do not fail to visit Blackroot Refreshment Rooms adjoining Blackroot Pool, an easy walk from the main entrance. First-class refreshments, mineral waters, ices, etc. Large and small parties catered for. Seating accommodation for 300. Open on Sundays.

Picnic parties supplied with tea.

Amusements include: fishing, a good fleet of rowing-boats, canoes, and motor launch, children's newly constructed boating and paddling-pool, with rowing-boats and paddle-boats, open spaces for games and delightful walks.

Please note only address :

BLACKROOT - SUTTON PARK
SUTTON COLDFIELD

Right: Advertisement for Blackroot Café.

Opposite below: '...Connected with the winter garden will be a long glass building, at the end of which will rise a large glazed dome ninety feet high, the glass being a quarter of an inch thick, and set in an ornamental iron framework. The floor of this part of the building, covered with Val de Travers asphalte, will form the skating rink, which will have a skating surface of 8,000 feet. Around the rink and overlooking the gardens will be a terrace promenade 150 yards in length. The aquarium will be underneath this part of the building, and will be fitted up with sixteen tanks for fish'.

CRYSTAL PALACE
SUTTON PARK.

CRYSTAL PALACE, SUTTON.

The ZOO ! The ZOO !

OPEN DAILY
9 a.m. till Dark.

Admission, 3d.
Children, 1d.

THE

ROYAL ZOOLOGICAL GARDENS,

CRYSTAL PALACE GROUNDS, SUTTON COLDFIELD.

SPECIAL ATTRACTIONS. _____

MONKEYS. MONKEYS. MONKEYS.

LIONS, BEARS, WOLVES, LEOPARDS, CAMELS,
ANTELOPES, KANGAROOS, and Hundreds of
other Novelties.

Special attention is called to the fact that this collection
is not a travelling Menagerie, but a Permanent Zoological
Gardens, open Summer and Winter, and consists of upwards
of 10 acres of Land and Water, filled with living specimens
of Natural History from all parts of the world, proving
both interesting, amusing and instructive, and the finest
place in the Midlands for a few hours' enjoyment.

Left: At the turn of the last century the site also
housed a zoo, which included large cats.

Below: The famous showman Pat Collins took
over the Crystal Palace in around 1910. The big
dipper was purchased from Southport by Mr
Collins and erected at the site. The structure
covered roughly an acre, with half a mile of track
and a maximum height of sixty feet.

Crystal Palace
Amusements Park

Operations proceeding for the Finest
Amusements Park in the Midlands.

Boating, Switchbacks Miniature
Railways, Grottos, Swings, etc.

CATERING for LARGE and
SMALL PARTIES UNDER COVER.
From one to one thousand five hundred
can be seated at once.

Special Terms for School Treats.

'Phone : 2192 Sutton Coldfield

Proprietor - - - Mr. P. COLLINS
General Manager - - R. H. DELANEY

Sutton Coldfield, Warwickshire

Advertisement for the Crystal Palace, 1935. It contained 350 tons of timber and machinery and took up to four trains at a time, each carrying thirty passengers. The structure was transported in 125 railway trucks and fifty men were employed to erect it. The dipper was eventually moved again, this time to Battersea Funfair in London.

The Crystal Palace swing boats and swing chairs in the background would seem very tame by today's modern fairground standards. However, in its day it was a top attraction.

In the early 1960s the Palace buildings deteriorated and the building was demolished in May 1962. The buildings had become very dilapidated but what a landmark the Crystal Palace would be today if it had survived.

The Sutton Miniature railway opened in June 1907, in the ground of the Crystal Palace. It was ten-and-a-half gauge, running from the Crystal Palace to a terminus at Wyndley Pool.

In 1908 major improvements included reconstructing the line in fifteen-inch gauge and making the track longer with run round loops at either end.

Some time after 1915 the railway fell into disuse but was re-opened by Pat Collins in 1922, this time with a circular route. The engine in this photograph is a 4-4-2, The Prince of Wales. The supporting framework of the 'Switchback Ride' at the Par Collins fairground can be seen in the background.

The 1938 station and booking office. The railway closed on 7 October 1962. After more than forty years in storage in Oldbury and a substantial grant from the Heritage Lottery fund the railway was moved, restored and reopened at the Cleethorpes Coast Light Railway in Lincolnshire.

Over the years Sutton Park has seen many forms of entertainment, including visits from the Bertram Mills Circus. They performed in the Park from Monday 7 July to Wednesday 9 July 1958.

BMC

PROGRAMME

MUSICAL DIRECTOR :
CHARLES HOTHAM, L.R.A.M.

EQUESTRIAN DIRECTORS :
A. YELDING and F. FOSTER, Jnr.

OVERTURE

CHARIVARI
Fun and Frolics as the buffoons take their bow.

THE MOHAWK INDIAN RIDERS
Yipeee, folks—it's bareback ridin' and rope spinnin' at its wild and woolly best !

PHYLLIS and her POODLES
Lucky Dogs ! If only we poor humans could derive as much pleasure from our work as these delightful poodles so evidently obtain from their lively romp in the ring.

THE GHEZZI TRIO
This is what Circus folk call a " Humpsti-bumpsti " act—it sounds full of bumps and bangs, and it is ! It isn't only the chairs and tables that get knocked about, either.

MILLS ARABIAN HORSES
A spirited team of Greys from the famous Mills Stables presented by Nadia Houcke.

FERRY FORST
Incredible, unbelievable Ferry Forst proves that the impossible is possible when his famous Company take the ring.

CLARINDA
Dancing and skipping on a galloping horse, with Oh ! such grace. Here is a reminder of the old-time circus brought glamorously to life.

MILLS FOUR BABY ELEPHANTS
A gay and attractive Elephant Revue in which the babies obviously are " hand-in-trunk " with their attractive partner.

INTERVAL
Ices and Refreshments are on sale in the Main Entrance.

CLOWNS AND AUGUSTES
A colourful cavalcade of crazy comics combining to convulse and captivate countless crowds, including Coco, Beppo, Little Billy, Nikki and Jackie Sloan.

THE CIRCUS PROGRAMME
WILL NOT BE TELEVISED

1958

**THE CIRCUS ANIMALS
and the MENAGERIE**
may be visited after each performance and daily from 11 a.m. until one hour before the commencement of the first performance. Do not fail to see the Baby Elephants, Lion Cubs, Tigers, Monkeys, Zebras, Llama, Donkeys, Arab Stallions and the huge collection of other animals from the four corners of the earth.

ALEX KERR and his TIGERS
Magnificent tigers handled in the modern manner with courage and understanding by a patient young Scot.

FRANCES DUNCAN
Aerial artistry with faultless timing and sheer pluck.

DUBROW'S DONKEY DERBY
Donkey Rides ? No thank you. Not when the animals concerned are members of Kurt Dubrow's unique troupe. The donkeys have a sense of humour all their own—so anything can happen !

THE TWO MASCOTTS
Unbelievable feats of head-to-head balancing performed with grace and courage by two charming sisters from Germany.

MILLS HIGH SCHOOL HORSES
A delightful display of equestrian elegance demonstrated by Phyllis Allan and Nadia Houcke.

COCO and CO.
Coco and Billy get jobs as nightwatchmen at a slightly haunted castle.

AFRICAN ZEBRAS with PALOMINOS and PONIES
Colourful, clever and charming; a masterpiece of animal training which took many months to bring to such perfection.

THE NEW DE RIAZ
The greatest aerial thrill in Circusdom performed by three gallant Parisiens.

GOD SAVE THE QUEEN

REDUCED PRICES for organised parties of 12 or more. Apply early to the Box Office for details.

THE SAME PERFORMANCE is given at the matinee, evening and last day performances, but the right is reserved to vary or curtail the programme in the event of unforeseen circumstances.

FOR YOUR INFORMATION

MOVING PICTURE CAMERAS ARE PROHIBITED
Ordinary cameras (without flashlight or tripod) may be used providing no disturbance or annoyance is caused to other members of the audience. Photographs taken may not be used for commercial purposes.

FOR LOST PROPERTY direct your enquiries to the lost property office in the vestibule on your left as you leave by the main entrance.

PHYSICIANS and others who anticipate being called during the performance are advised to inform the House Manager at the Main Entrance of their seat numbers in order that messages may be conveyed promptly.

Right: Alex Kerr's Tiger Act, 9 July 1958. It is said that Alex Kerr took one of his tigers on a lead for daily walks in the Park. (Dr John Raines)

Below: Henry Lewandowski at Town Gate, 7 July 1958. Henry Lewandowski's bicycle was eight feet high. Here he is returning from a publicity ride along the Parade in the town. Note the park keeper's bicycle clips: perhaps he thought he could patrol the Park more effectively from the height of the eight feet high bicycle. (Dr John Raines)

Opposite above: The Big Top of the Bertram Mills Circus, 7 July 1958. The big top was situated on the area to the left of the road leading from Town Gate, immediately beyond the bridge over the paddling stream. (Dr John Raines)

Opposite below: The circus would not be acceptable today but in 1958 people would have been entertained by Ferry Frost the German Illusionist, the Mohawk Indian riders, Phyllis and her poodles, the Mills Arabian horses, the Two Sisters – the two mascots who performed balancing acts – African zebras with the palomino ponies, Clarinda, a bareback rider, the Ghezzi Trio, who performed a 'Humpsti-bumpsti' act, and Coco & Co. the clowns. (Dr John Raines)

Above: Sutton Coldfield Cine Society making a film in Sutton Park, 1945.

Left: The RAC Rally first used Sutton Park as one of its stages in 1972. It always used to be on a Saturday but was moved to Sundays because of spectator safety reasons. In 1979 crowd of over 12,000 watched the cars speed through the Park. The ford at Wyndley was always a popular place for watching. In 1986 the Local Authority proposed to charge entry into the Park to watch the rally when it realized what a real money-spinner it would be.

With the safety factor dictating that the rally should only use the Park in daylight hours, and the growing concerns about the damage done during the event, Birmingham City Council finally said 'no' to the organisers using Sutton Park after the 1993 event.

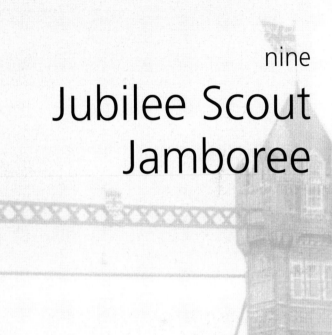

nine

Jubilee Scout Jamboree

Aerial view of the camp. The World Scout Jubilee Jamboree was a unique gathering of Scouts from all parts of the world. It comprised of a World Scout Jamboree, a World Rover Moot and a World Scouters Indaba. Never before had the three events been held at the same place and at the same time. The Jamboree was a major world celebration of Baden-Powell's birthday centenary and the golden jubilee of the worldwide movement he founded. The purpose of all Jamborees, Rover Moots and Scouters Indabas was to provide an opportunity for the Scouts of different countries to meet and make individual friendships, so strengthening the bonds of the Scout brotherhood.

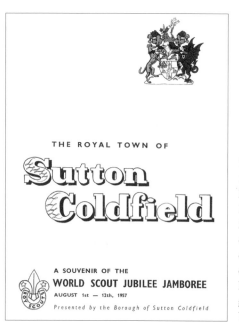

THE ROYAL TOWN OF

Sutton Coldfield

A SOUVENIR OF THE
WORLD SCOUT JUBILEE JAMBOREE
AUGUST 1st — 12th, 1957
Presented by the Borough of Sutton Coldfield

The first World Jamboree was held at Olympia in 1920, followed by Copenhagen (1924), Arrowe Park, Birkenhead (1929), the Royal Forest at Godallo, Hungary (1933), Vogelenzang, Holland (1937), Moission, France (1947), Austria (1951) and Nigeria-on-the-Lake, Canada in 1955. It was in the summer of 1953 that the Boy Scouts International Conference decided to celebrate fifty years of Scouting with the holding of a hitherto untried combined international gathering, and the Boy Scout Association of the United Kingdom was invited to organize the event.

118

Archway near Town Gate, 10 August 1957. Suggestions and offers came from numerous places around the country that wished to hold the event. A shortlist was drawn up and in 1954 the selectors paid a visit to Sutton Park. The citizens of Sutton Coldfield were justifiably proud when the Park was offered the task of holding the JIM, the Jubilee Jamboree, Indaba and Moot. (Dr John Raines)

Outline Programme of the Jamboree

Monday, 29th July—British Contingent takes up residence in Sutton Park.

Tuesday, 30th July Overseas and foreign Contingents arrive and
Wednesday, 31st July settle in.

Thursday, 1st August—Opening Ceremony in the Arena.

Friday, 2nd August—Visit of Girl Guides from their International Camp at Windsor; Arena Displays (afternoon); Camp Theatre and Open Air Cinema (evening).

Saturday, 3rd August—Air Scout Display in Arena (afternoon); Camp Theatre (evening); Arena Show by non-Scout body or bodies (evening).

Sunday, 4th August—International Scouts' Own Service, Arena (morning); Pontifical High Mass (morning); International Tea Parties (afternoon); Community Hymn Singing in the Arena (evening).

Monday, 5th August—Arena Displays (afternoon); Camp Theatre (evening); Arena Shows by non-Scout bodies (evening).

Tuesday, 6th August—Arena Displays (afternoon); Camp Theatre and
(Wolf Cub Day). Open Air Cinema (evening).

Wednesday, 7th August—Arena Displays (afternoon); Camp Theatre and Open Air Cinema (evening).

Thursday, 8th August—Arena Displays (afternoon); Camp Theatre (evening); Arena Show by non-Scout bodies (evening).

Friday, 9th August—United Kingdom Contingent Show in Arena (afternoon); Camp Theatre and Open Air Cinema (evening).

Saturday, 10th August—Sea Scout Display on Powells Pool (afternoon); Arena Display (afternoon); Camp Theatre (evening).

Sunday, 11th August—Religious Observances (morning); United Kingdom at Home to the World (afternoon); Community Hymn Singing (evening).

Monday, 12th August—Closing Ceremony (evening).

26

Programme of events. Jamboree was the name given by Baden-Powell to the first international gathering of Scouts at Olympia in 1920. When asked 'why jamboree?' he is said to have replied 'what else could you call it?' Indaba means a gathering of the chiefs. The first World Indaba was held at Gilwell Park in Essex in 1952. 'Moot' was again a suggestion by Baden-Powell. It comes from an old English word meaning a gathering of young men for discussion concerning the affairs of the community.

Flowerbed to commemorate the Jamboree. Planning for the event commenced in the spring of 1955 when the Directing Committee was formed. Under the direction of the Assistant Organising Commissioners, sub-committees responsible for the various services were built up whilst in the Midlands a body of people formed themselves into other sub-committees to tackle on the spot problems arising from catering, contracts, transport, publicity, health, excursions and hospitality.

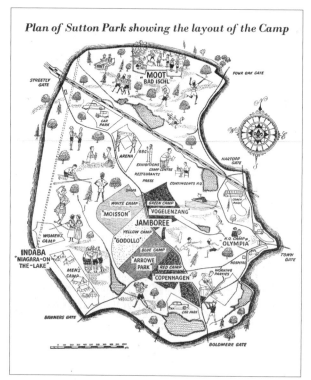

Plan of Sutton Park showing the layout of the camps. Over a period of two years a voluntary army of over 5,000 people were formed to organize the event. To ensure that the huge camp would be properly serviced and the participants adequately fed and entertained the organisers found themselves faced with an expenditure of over £500,000. It would have been much more but for the generosity of British firms and the Government, who either loaned equipment or supplied materials.

Only those faced with the organisation could fully appreciate the numerous and varied problems they faced. For example, whilst the sandy soil of Sutton Park ensured excellent drainage, it did not allow for the widespread movement of heavy transport. Existing roads had to be supplemented with a number of temporary byways, all of which had to be removed. The usual form of camp sanitation could not be carried out owing to the danger of collapsing soil. For the first time at a Jamboree, an elaborate system of automatic water-borne toilets piped into the town's permanent sewage network was installed.

This too was the first time that three international events catering for large numbers and both sexes had been attempted. Flood lighting and road illuminations, large-scale exhibitions, a fully equipped theatre and covered grandstands capable of holding 15,000 spectators had to be built - just a few of the problem the committees were faced with.

Above: Vogelenzang Sub-Camp Gateway, 12 August 1957. The Jamboree was attended by 31,000 Scouts from 85 countries. They came from: Aden (210), Argentina (1), Australia (169), Barbados (30), Belgium (1,508), Brazil (59), Canada (1,470), Cuba (53), Germany (2,000), Greece (2), Hong Kong (21), Iran (114), Italy (1,651), Leeward Islands (4), Libya (5), Mexico (30), New Zealand (190), Sarawak (21), South Africa (380), Turkey (24), United Kingdom (9,844), United States of America (1,759), United Nations (1), and many more. (Dr John Raines)

Left: London Contingent Gateway, 12 August 1957. Participants and visitors arrived by various forms of transport. Scouts arrived by boats, ten ports were used, twenty-two countries arrived by plane, three Scoutmasters from Brazil road-tested a jeep, and the Iranians drove their own buses overland: 190 of the 830 Austrian contingent arrived by cycle and motorcycle. British Rail undertook the bulk of the travel arrangements. Over one million visitors were to visit the Jamboree and British Rail put on 266 special trains. (Dr John Raines)

Above: The Queen and Duke touring the camp. The event was officially opened by the Duke of Gloucester, who was president of the Boy Scout Association. The opening ceremony took place on 1 August 1957 and at 3 p.m. he declared the Jubilee Jamboree, Indaba and Moot officially open to 30,000 Scouts in formation and approximately 100,000 visitors.

Right: The Order of Ceremony for the Royal Visit. The Queen arrived to visit the event on 3 August. As royal patron of the British Boy Scout Association, she and HRH Prince Philip, patron of the Baden-Powell Scout Guild, spent six hours with the Scouts in the Park, after being welcomed by the mayor of Sutton Coldfield, Kathleen Smith.

THE ROYAL TOWN OF SUTTON COLDFIELD

Order of Ceremony

that will be performed at the

CIVIC RECEPTION at the TOWN HALL

to

Her Majesty The Queen

and

His Royal Highness The Prince Philip,
The Duke of Edinburgh

on the occasion of their visit to the

WORLD SCOUT JUBILEE JAMBOREE

Sutton Park, Sutton Coldfield

Warwickshire

Saturday, 3 August, 1957

Sarawak Contingent Gateway, 10 August 1957. The food bill for the Jamboree came to £160,000. During the twelve days 2,170,000 meals were prepared by the couts themselves, in addition to snacks. Just some of the items on the shopping list: 40 tons of fresh meat, 486,600 eggs, 540,000 pints of milk, 432,000 bread rolls, 274,000 large loaves of bread, 16 tons of butter, 31 tons of sausages, 40 tons of sugar, 4.5 tons of tea, 14 tons of coffee, 40,500 bottles of sauce, 40 tons of fresh fruit and 15 hundredweight of prunes. (Dr John Raines)

Copenhagen Sub-Camp Gateway, 10 August 1957. The camp had all the amenities of a medium-sized town. The camp centre comprised a shopping area supplying everything from a tent peg to a newspaper to an aspirin. The site had seven banks and its own telephone exchange – telephone number Jubilee 7711. Huge water tanks, which had a capacity of 250,000 gallons, supplied the 500,000 gallons of water used each day. More than twenty miles of pipeline were laid. Each sub-camp had its own medical inspection room and first-aid post. The camp hospital was loaned by the Royal Air Force and contained 300 beds in ten wards; a mobile dental clinic was also stationed in the Park. The camp had its own refuse collection vehicle and an SOS for the loan of 1,200 dustbins was answered. The site also had its own Scout police and fire service. (Dr John Raines)

South Africa Contingent Gateway, 12 August 1957. A fully equipped press camp was kept busy with accommodation for the press, radio and television. A 16mm colour and sound film recording of the Jamboree was taken and is available for loan on video (and by 2006, hopefully on DVD) from Sutton Coldfield Reference Library. A twelve to sixteen page daily newspaper was published entitled *Jubilee Journal*. The eleven editions cost 6d each. Pity the newspaper boys who delivered to an estimated 40,000 inside the camp alone, delivering the editions in time for breakfast each morning. (Dr John Raines)

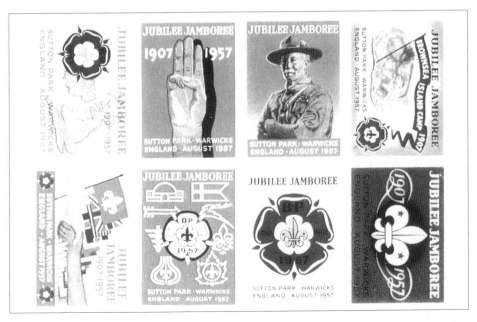

The GPO issued three special postage stamps to commemorate the event. It was the first time that Great Britain had issued a special stamp for a World Scout Jamboree. The stamps cost 2½d for inland letter rate, 4d for foreign letter rate and 1s 3d for normal airmail letter rate.

Moisson Sub-Camp Gateway, 10 August 1957.
Lady Baden-Powell closed the Jamboree on 12
August 1957, with the words 'the end is only
the beginning'. All spectators and every Scout
flocked to the area for the closing speeches.
As the lights dimmed they were treated to a
brilliant firework display. (Dr John Raines)

British Guiana Contingent Gateway, 10 August
1957. The tremendous volume of prolonged
cheers gave way to the strains of the Jamboree
song as the Scouts spontaneously formed
themselves into international groups, linked
arms and marched away from the arena for the
last time. (Dr John Raines.)

Right: This event, which hosted over 31,000 Scouts from some eighty-five countries, is commemorated by the Jamboree Memorial Stone, which can be found within the triangle formed by the road junction north of Keeper's Pool and the road from Streetly Gate. The Park itself recovered from the thousands of pairs of feet which walked all over it, and Memorial Stone and the Jamboree Plantation serve as reminders of the event.

Below: Pendants, badges and passes for the event in 1957. These belonged to Norman G. Evans, one of the camp dentists and a former local historian of Sutton Coldfield. The year 2007 will see the fiftieth anniversary of this tremendous event, with celebrations taking place all over the city, and in fact the country. Many of the Scouts who attended the event fifty years ago will be travelling from all over the world to renew acquaintances.

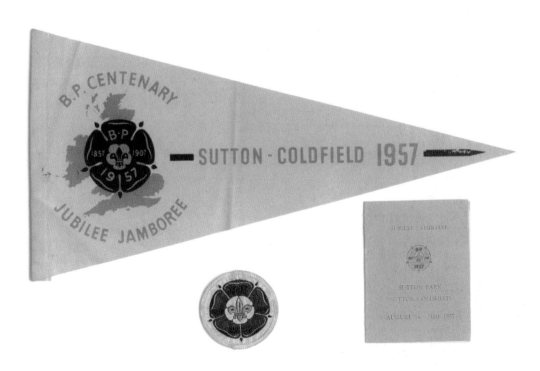

Other local titles published by Tempus

Haunted Birmingham
ARTHUR SMITH AND RACHEL BANNISTER

From creepy accounts of the city centre to phantoms of the theatre, haunted pubs and hospitals, *Haunted Birmingham* contains a chilling range of ghostly phenomena. Drawing on historical and contemporary sources, you will hear about the landlady who haunts the site of her death, the two workmen who died during the building of the Town Hall, the late mayor who still watches over the city, the last man to be publicly hanged in Birmingham, and many more ghostly goings–on.

0-7524-4017-9

Central Birmingham Pubs Volume I
JOSEPH MCKENNA

This fascinating volume records the pubs, inns, taverns and beerhouses of the central city, an area now within the present Inner Ring Road and the Bull Ring. This is the very heart of the city and although it comprises only one square mile and can be crossed by foot in less than half an hour, it is an area that has seen over 760 pubs – all of which are faithfully recorded here.

0-7524-3873-5

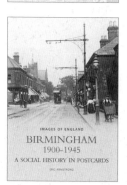

Birmingham The Building of a City
JOSEPH MCKENNA

Since the time of William Hutton's history of Birmingham in 1780, there has been no real attempt to describe and explain the physical growth of Birmingham as a city and to consider why it developed in the way it did. When was the growth and why did it occur? What created the city street plans we see today? Who were the men who designed, financed and built modern Birmingham? This fascinating book provides answers to these important questions and more.

0-7524-3489-6

Birmingham 1900-1945 A Social History in Postcards
ERIC ARMSTRONG

This fascinating collection of over 200 picture postcards provides a nostalgic insight into the changing history of Birmingham during the period 1900-1945. Each image brings the past alive, describing many aspects of life in the city, including wartime, work, sport, shopping, entertainment and celebrations. This book will appeal to anyone with an interest in the history of the area, and also awaken memories of a bygone time for those who worked or lived in the 'Second City'.

0-7524-4037-3

If you are interested in purchasing other books published by Tempus, or in case you have difficulty finding any Tempus books in your local bookshop, you can also place orders directly through our website

www.tempus-publishing.com